Mason Jar Morning Meals: 50 Mason Jar Breakfast Recipes That Are Quick, Healthy and Great on the Go

Table of Contents

Gluten-free pancakes 95

Smoothie Based Recipes

Pink smoothie

Serves: 2

Time: 2 minutes

Ingredients:

- ½ tablespoon flax seeds
- 2 tablespoons oatmeal
- 1 tablespoon chia seeds
- 1 tablespoon protein powder
- ½ cup strawberries
- ¼ cup beets, cooked and diced
- ½ banana, frozen, sliced
- 4 tablespoons Greek yogurt
- 1 cup almond milk

Directions:

1. Place oats, flax seeds and chia seeds in a standard Mason jar.
2. Unscrew the base from your blender pitcher and apply onto Mason jar. I will fit perfectly if you are using standard jar.
3. Process for 30 seconds.
4. Carefully remove and add remaining ingredients. Apply the jar onto base and process until you get perfectly smooth mixture.
5. Serve immediately.

Nutrition Facts

Serving Size 217 g

Amount Per Serving

Calories 366	Calories from Fat 279
	% Daily Value*
Total Fat 31.0g	48%
Saturated Fat 25.7g	128%
Trans Fat 0.0g	
Cholesterol 0mg	0%
Sodium 36mg	1%
Potassium 599mg	17%
Total Carbohydrates 23.7g	8%
Dietary Fiber 6.8g	27%
Sugars 11.2g	
Protein 5.4g	

Vitamin A 1%	•	Vitamin C 47%
Calcium 6%	•	Iron 19%

Nutrition Grade B-

* Based on a 2000 calorie diet

Peach-coconut smoothie

Serves: 2

Time: 5 minutes

Ingredients:

- 1 cup coconut milk, chilled
- 2 peaches, stoned, peeled and cut into chunks
- ½ cup ice
- ¼ teaspoon cinnamon, ground

Directions:

1. Add coconut milk, ice, peaches and cinnamon in Mason jar.
2. Unscrew the base from your blender pitcher and apply onto Mason jar. I will fit perfectly if you are using standard jar.
3. Fit the jar onto blender and blend for 30 seconds.
4. Serve immediately.

Nutrition Facts

Serving Size 280 g

Amount Per Serving

Calories 100	Calories from Fat 25

	% Daily Value*
Total Fat 2.8g	4%
Saturated Fat 1.5g	8%
Trans Fat 0.0g	
Cholesterol 10mg	3%
Sodium 59mg	2%
Potassium 258mg	7%
Total Carbohydrates 15.6g	5%
Dietary Fiber 1.6g	6%
Sugars 13.7g	
Protein 4.9g	

Vitamin A 7%	•	Vitamin C 11%	
Calcium 16%	•	Iron 2%	

Nutrition Grade B+

* Based on a 2000 calorie diet

Strawberry-nut smoothie

Serves: 1

Time: 3 minutes

Ingredients:

- ½ banana, medium, sliced
- ¾ cup milk
- 1 cup strawberries, frozen
- 1 tablespoon almond butter
- 1 tablespoon honey

Directions:

1. Place all ingredients in a Mason jar.
2. Unscrew the base from your blender pitcher and apply onto standard Mason jar.
3. Fit the jar onto blender and blend for 1 minute or until smooth.
4. Serve immediately.

Nutrition Facts

Serving Size 423 g

Amount Per Serving

Calories 356	Calories from Fat 121	
		% Daily Value*
Total Fat 13.4g		21%
Saturated Fat 3.2g		16%
Cholesterol 15mg		5%
Sodium 89mg		4%
Potassium 669mg		19%
Total Carbohydrates 53.7g		18%
Dietary Fiber 5.0g		20%
Sugars 39.8g		
Protein 11.1g		
Vitamin A 2%	•	Vitamin C 150%
Calcium 29%	•	Iron 8%

Nutrition Grade B+

* Based on a 2000 calorie diet

Mango smoothie

Serves: 1

Time: 2 minutes

Ingredients:

- ½ cup milk
- 1 cup mango, chopped
- ½ cup ice
- ¼ cup yogurt
- 1 tablespoon honey

Directions:

1. Place all ingredients in Mason jar.
2. Unscrew the base from your blender pitcher and apply onto standard Mason jar.
3. Fit the jar onto blender and blend for 40 seconds until frothy.
4. Serve immediately.

Nutrition Facts

Serving Size 423 g

Amount Per Serving

Calories 1,935   Calories from Fat 89

	% Daily Value*
Total Fat 9.9g	15%
Saturated Fat 2.1g	11%
Cholesterol 14mg	5%
Sodium 105mg	4%
Potassium 4608mg	132%
Total Carbohydrates 507.6g	169%
Dietary Fiber 53.4g	213%
Sugars 450.4g	
Protein 20.9g	

Vitamin A 45%	•	Vitamin C 2279%
Calcium 30%	•	Iron 1%

Nutrition Grade A

* Based on a 2000 calorie diet

Peanut-espresso smoothie

Serves: 1

Time: 2 minutes

Ingredients:

- ½ teaspoon instant espresso powder
- ½ cup ice
- ½ cup milk
- 2 tablespoons creamy peanut butter
- ½ banana, medium, sliced

Directions:

1. Place all ingredients in Mason jar.
2. Apply a blender base onto standard Mason jar and fit the jar onto blender.
3. Process for 20 seconds and serve immediately.

Nutrition Facts

Serving Size 333 g

Amount Per Serving

Calories 302	Calories from Fat 169
	% Daily Value*
Total Fat 18.8g	29%
Saturated Fat 5.0g	25%
Cholesterol 10mg	3%
Sodium 209mg	9%
Potassium 490mg	14%
Total Carbohydrates 25.8g	9%
Dietary Fiber 3.4g	14%
Sugars 15.7g	
Protein 12.6g	

Vitamin A 1%	•	Vitamin C 9%
Calcium 15%	•	Iron 18%

Nutrition Grade B-

* Based on a 2000 calorie diet

Oatmeal-strawberry smoothie

Serves: 2

Time: 3 minutes

Ingredients:

- 1 cup milk
- ½ cup rolled oats
- 14 strawberries, frozen
- 2 teaspoons honey
- 1 banana, sliced
- ¼ teaspoon vanilla extract
- Few ice cubes

Directions:

1. Place ingredients, by order in a Mason jar.
2. Unscrew the base from your blender pitcher and apply onto standard Mason jar.
3. Fit the jar onto blender and process until smooth.
4. Serve after.

Nutrition Facts

Serving Size 293 g

Amount Per Serving

Calories 241	Calories from Fat 38

	% Daily Value*
Total Fat 4.3g	7%
Saturated Fat 1.8g	9%
Cholesterol 10mg	3%
Sodium 60mg	3%
Potassium 488mg	14%
Total Carbohydrates 45.6g	15%
Dietary Fiber 5.3g	21%
Sugars 22.9g	
Protein 7.9g	

Vitamin A 2%	Vitamin C 91%
Calcium 17%	Iron 8%

Nutrition Grade B

* Based on a 2000 calorie diet

Chia-raspberry smoothie

Serves: 1

Time: 4 minutes

Ingredients:

- 1/3 cup raspberries, frozen
- 1/3 cup milk
- 1/3 cup yogurt
- 2 teaspoons chia seeds
- 1 tablespoon honey
- ¼ cup blanched almonds, divided

Directions:

1. Reserve few almonds and raspberries to garnish.
2. Place remaining ingredients in a Mason jar.
3. Apply the blender pitcher base onto Mason jar.
4. Fit the jar onto blender and process for 3 minutes or until smooth.
5. Garnish with reserved almonds and raspberries before serving.

Nutrition Facts

Serving Size 254 g

Amount Per Serving

Calories 341	Calories from Fat 148

	% Daily Value*
Total Fat 16.5g	25%
Saturated Fat 2.9g	14%
Trans Fat 0.0g	
Cholesterol 12mg	4%
Sodium 97mg	4%
Potassium 518mg	15%
Total Carbohydrates 39.0g	13%
Dietary Fiber 7.3g	29%
Sugars 29.5g	
Protein 13.9g	

Vitamin A 1%	•	Vitamin C 20%
Calcium 36%	•	Iron 10%

Nutrition Grade A

* Based on a 2000 calorie diet

Blueberry flax smoothie

Serves: 1

Time: 3 minutes

Ingredients:

- 3 oz. yogurt
- ½ banana, medium, sliced
- ½ cup blueberries, fresh or frozen
- ½ tablespoon honey
- ½ tablespoon flax seeds, ground
- ½ cup milk
- ¼ cup ice cubes

Directions:

1. Place all ingredients in a standard Mason jar.
2. Apply blender base onto jar and fit the jar on a blender.
3. Blend ingredients until smooth.
4. Continue blending for 60 seconds more to add air which will make smoothie lighter.
5. Serve immediately.

Nutrition Facts

Serving Size 412 g

Amount Per Serving

Calories 266	Calories from Fat 46

	% Daily Value*
Total Fat 5.1g	8%
Saturated Fat 2.6g	13%
Trans Fat 0.0g	
Cholesterol 15mg	5%
Sodium 121mg	5%
Potassium 571mg	16%
Total Carbohydrates 45.6g	15%
Dietary Fiber 4.2g	17%
Sugars 34.6g	
Protein 10.7g	

Vitamin A 2%	•	Vitamin C 29%
Calcium 31%	•	Iron 13%

Nutrition Grade A-

* Based on a 2000 calorie diet

Like-a-pina-colada smoothie

Serves: 1

Time: 3 minutes

Ingredients:

- 2 tablespoons oats
- ¼ banana, medium, sliced
- ¼ cup coconut milk
- ¼ cup pineapple chunks
- 2.5oz. thick, Greek style yogurt

Directions:

1. Place oats, banana and pineapple chunks in a Mason jar.
2. Add thick yogurt and pour over coconut milk.
3. Apply blender base onto Mason jar and fit the jar on the blender.
4. Pulse until smooth, for 60 seconds.
5. Serve after.

Nutrition Facts

Serving Size 212 g

Amount Per Serving

Calories 266	Calories from Fat 136

% Daily Value*

Total Fat 15.1g	23%
Saturated Fat 12.8g	64%
Trans Fat 0.0g	
Cholesterol 5mg	2%
Sodium 43mg	2%
Potassium 345mg	10%
Total Carbohydrates 25.7g	9%
Dietary Fiber 3.7g	15%
Sugars 11.7g	
Protein 10.3g	

Vitamin A 1%	•	Vitamin C 40%
Calcium 9%	•	Iron 9%

Nutrition Grade B

* Based on a 2000 calorie diet

Creamy breakfast smoothie

Serves: 1

Time: 2 minutes

Ingredients:

- 1 peach, large
- 1 cup milk
- 1small pinch cinnamon (preferably Ceylon)
- ½ cup yogurt
- ¼ teaspoon vanilla extract
- Handful of ice cubes

Directions:

1. Remove stone from the peach and slice it thinly.
2. Place the peach in a Mason jar and add remaining ingredients.
3. Unscrew the base from your blender pitcher and apply onto standard Mason jar.
4. Fit the jar onto blender and process until smooth, for 60 seconds.
5. Serve after.

Nutrition Facts

Serving Size 466 g

Amount Per Serving

Calories 251 | Calories from Fat 61

% Daily Value*

Total Fat 6.8g	10%
Saturated Fat 4.2g	21%
Trans Fat 0.0g	
Cholesterol 27mg	9%
Sodium 201mg	8%
Potassium 616mg	18%
Total Carbohydrates 30.3g	10%
Dietary Fiber 1.6g	6%
Sugars 28.0g	
Protein 15.9g	

Vitamin A 9%	•	Vitamin C 12%
Calcium 52%	•	Iron 2%

Nutrition Grade C+

* Based on a 2000 calorie diet

Oatmeal Based Recipes

Creamy strawberry-vanilla oatmeal

Serves: 2

Time: 5 minutes + overnight time

Ingredients:

For the strawberry jam:

- 1 cup strawberries, fresh
- 2 tablespoons chia seeds
- 1 tablespoon honey, raw

For the oatmeal:

- 2 cups milk
- 2 cups rolled oats
- ½ tablespoon pure vanilla extract
- 2 tablespoons chia seeds

Directions:

1. In a large Mason jar combine strawberries and honey.
2. Using a fork mash strawberries until you get a nice puree. Add chia seeds and stir well.
3. Add in rolled oats, milk, vanilla and remaining chia seeds; cover and store in refrigerator overnight.
4. In the morning stir oats with prepared strawberry jam and enjoy.

Nutrition Facts

Serving Size 427 g

Amount Per Serving

Calories 554	Calories from Fat 140

	% Daily Value*
Total Fat 15.6g	24%
Saturated Fat 4.3g	22%
Trans Fat 0.0g	
Cholesterol 20mg	7%
Sodium 121mg	5%
Potassium 656mg	19%
Total Carbohydrates 88.0g	29%
Dietary Fiber 14.7g	59%
Sugars 24.4g	
Protein 22.3g	

Vitamin A 1%	•	Vitamin C 72%
Calcium 47%	•	Iron 28%

Nutrition Grade B+

* Based on a 2000 calorie diet

Peanut butter oatmeal

Serves: 2

Time: 5 minutes + inactive time

Ingredients:

- ½ cup rolled oats
- ½ cup milk
- ½ cup peanut butter
- 2 tablespoons brown sugar
- ½ cup Greek yogurt
- ½ teaspoon vanilla extract
- 2 tablespoons raspberry jam

Directions:

1. Place the oats in a jar; sprinkle with brown sugar, evenly and add peanut butter.
2. In separate bowl whisk the milk, yogurt and vanilla. Pour over rolled oats.
3. Close with the lid and shake vigorously.
4. Store in a fridge overnight. In the morning add the raspberry jam and swirl it over oats.
5. You can reheat oats in microwave and serve after.

Nutrition Facts

Serving Size 171 g

Amount Per Serving

Calories 574	Calories from Fat 315

	% Daily Value*
Total Fat 35.0g	54%
Saturated Fat 7.8g	39%
Cholesterol 5mg	2%
Sodium 329mg	14%
Potassium 541mg	15%
Total Carbohydrates 51.5g	17%
Dietary Fiber 5.9g	24%
Sugars 26.9g	
Protein 20.9g	

Vitamin A 0%	•	Vitamin C 0%
Calcium 9%	•	Iron 39%

Nutrition Grade C+

* Based on a 2000 calorie diet

Banana overnight oatmeal

Serves: 2

Time: 5 minutes + overnight time

Ingredients:

- 1 banana, medium, sliced
- 1/3 cup rolled oats
- 1 tablespoon chia seeds
- ¾ cup milk
- 1 fig, ripe, finely chopped
- 2 tablespoons toasted almonds flakes
- 2 teaspoons light honey

Directions:

1. Combine milk, oats, chia seeds, honey and fig in large Mason jar.
2. Cover and store in refrigerator overnight.
3. In the morning garnish with banana and almonds flakes.
4. Serve after.

Nutrition Facts

Serving Size 277 g

Amount Per Serving

Calories 252	Calories from Fat 39

	% Daily Value*
Total Fat 4.3g	7%
Saturated Fat 1.5g	7%
Trans Fat 0.0g	
Cholesterol 8mg	3%
Sodium 45mg	2%
Potassium 403mg	12%
Total Carbohydrates 51.8g	17%
Dietary Fiber 5.1g	20%
Sugars 32.0g	
Protein 6.5g	

Vitamin A 1%	•	Vitamin C 9%
Calcium 16%	•	Iron 7%

Nutrition Grade B+

* Based on a 2000 calorie diet

Pumpkin oatmeal

Serves: 1

Time: 5 minutes + overnight time

Ingredients:

- ½ cup milk
- ¼ cup pumpkin puree
- ½ cup rolled oats
- Dash of cinnamon
- Dash of nutmeg
- Dash of cardamom

Directions:

1. Mix ingredients in standard Mason jar.
2. Cover and refrigerate overnight.
3. Serve in the morning, cold or you can even microwave for few minutes.
4. Stir once again and enjoy.

Nutrition Facts

Serving Size 225 g

Amount Per Serving

Calories 240	Calories from Fat 49

	% Daily Value*
Total Fat 5.5g	8%
Saturated Fat 2.1g	11%
Trans Fat 0.0g	
Cholesterol 10mg	3%
Sodium 63mg	3%
Potassium 349mg	10%
Total Carbohydrates 39.2g	13%
Dietary Fiber 6.2g	25%
Sugars 8.0g	
Protein 10.1g	

Vitamin A 191%	•	Vitamin C 4%	
Calcium 19%	•	Iron 15%	

Nutrition Grade A
* Based on a 2000 calorie diet

Orange oats

Serves: 1

Time: 3 minutes + overnight time

Ingredients:

- 1 tablespoon shredded coconut, toasted lightly
- 1/2 cup rolled oats
- 1 tablespoon pumpkin seeds
- ¼ teaspoon pure vanilla extract
- ¼ cup orange juice, fresh squeezed
- ½ orange, medium, sliced – to garnish

Directions:

1. Mix oats with vanilla, pumpkin seeds and orange juice in standard Mason jar.
2. Pour over water and refrigerate overnight.
3. In the morning stir the oats and top with shredded coconut and fresh orange slices.

Nutrition Facts

Serving Size 277 g

Amount Per Serving

Calories 340	Calories from Fat 112

	% Daily Value*
Total Fat 12.5g	19%
Saturated Fat 3.5g	17%
Cholesterol 0mg	0%
Sodium 9mg	0%
Potassium 598mg	17%
Total Carbohydrates 48.9g	16%
Dietary Fiber 7.6g	30%
Sugars 14.8g	
Protein 11.1g	

Vitamin A 6%	•	Vitamin C 169%	
Calcium 7%	•	Iron 33%	

Nutrition Grade B

* Based on a 2000 calorie diet

Choco oats

Serves: 1

Time: 3 minutes + overnight time

Ingredients:

- 1 cup water, boiling
- ½ cup rolled oats
- 1 tablespoon bulgur
- 1 tablespoon buckwheat groats
- 1 tablespoon millet
- 1 ½ tablespoons cocoa, raw
- ½ banana, medium, sliced
- 1 tablespoon chia seeds
- ¼ cup milk
- 1 tablespoon carob chips – to garnish

Directions:

1. Place rolled oats, bulgur, buckwheat, millet and cocoa powder in standard Mason jar.
2. Pour over boiling water and stir to combine, until cocoa is dissolved.
3. Cover and refrigerate overnight.
4. In the morning stir in the milk and banana puree.
5. Top with carob chips before serving.

Nutrition Facts

Serving Size 440 g

Amount Per Serving	
Calories 381	Calories from Fat 74

	% Daily Value*
Total Fat 8.2g	13%
Saturated Fat 2.0g	10%
Trans Fat 0.0g	
Cholesterol 5mg	2%
Sodium 43mg	2%
Potassium 685mg	20%
Total Carbohydrates 71.2g	24%
Dietary Fiber 13.2g	53%
Sugars 10.7g	
Protein 13.9g	

Vitamin A 1%	•	Vitamin C 9%
Calcium 18%	•	Iron 24%

Nutrition Grade A

* Based on a 2000 calorie diet

Peanut butter and maple oats

Serves: 1

Time: 3 minutes + overnight time

Ingredients:

- ¼ cup rolled oats
- ¾ cup milk
- 1 tablespoon chia seeds
- 1 teaspoon maple syrup
- ½ banana, medium, sliced
- 1 tablespoon peanut butter
- ½ teaspoon cinnamon
- 1 tablespoon chopped pecan nuts, toasted
- ¼ teaspoon pure vanilla

Directions:

1. In a standard Mason jar combine milk, oats, chia seeds, cinnamon and vanilla. Give it a good stir and cover.
2. Store in refrigerator overnight.
3. In the morning top oats with bananas and peanut butter.
4. Microwave for 15 seconds and drizzle with maple syrup just before serving.
5. Stir once again and enjoy.

Nutrition Facts

Serving Size 294 g

Amount Per Serving

Calories 365	Calories from Fat 143
	% Daily Value*
Total Fat 15.8g	24%
Saturated Fat 4.5g	22%
Trans Fat 0.0g	
Cholesterol 15mg	5%
Sodium 162mg	7%
Potassium 562mg	16%
Total Carbohydrates 47.9g	16%
Dietary Fiber 7.7g	31%
Sugars 21.2g	
Protein 14.9g	

Vitamin A 2%	•	Vitamin C 9%
Calcium 31%	•	Iron 19%

Nutrition Grade A-

* Based on a 2000 calorie diet

Superfood oatmeal

Serves: 1

Time: 3 minutes + overnight time

Ingredients:

- ¼ cup rolled oats
- ¾ cup almond milk
- 2 teaspoons cacao nibs
- 1 teaspoon chia seeds
- 1 tablespoon Goji berries
- 1 teaspoon hemp seeds
- 1 teaspoon honey

Directions:

1. Combine oats, milk, cacao nibs, Goji berries, hemp seeds and honey in standard Mason jar.
2. Apply the lid and shake well.
3. Store in refrigerator overnight.
4. In the morning reheat in microwave for 50 seconds before serving.

Nutrition Facts

Serving Size 231 g

Amount Per Serving

Calories 278	Calories from Fat 75

	% Daily Value*
Total Fat 8.3g	13%
Saturated Fat 2.7g	14%
Trans Fat 0.0g	
Cholesterol 15mg	5%
Sodium 88mg	4%
Potassium 239mg	7%
Total Carbohydrates 43.1g	14%
Dietary Fiber 4.7g	19%
Sugars 25.7g	
Protein 10.9g	

Vitamin A 3%	•	Vitamin C 18%
Calcium 25%	•	Iron 44%

Nutrition Grade B+

* Based on a 2000 calorie diet

Blueberry-banana oats

Serves: 1

Time: 5 minutes + overnight time

Ingredients:

- ½ cup Greek yogurt
- ½ cup almond milk
- ½ cup rolled oats
- ½ banana, medium, sliced
- ¼ cup blueberries, fresh
- 1 tablespoon favorite granola
- 2 teaspoons maple syrup

Directions:

1. Place banana slices and blueberries in standard Mason jar.
2. Using fork mash until blended.
3. Add oats, yogurt and milk and give it a good stir,
4. Cover and store in refrigerator overnight.
5. In the morning top with favorite granola and drizzle with maple syrup.
6. Serve after.

Nutrition Facts

Serving Size 285 g

Amount Per Serving

Calories 557	Calories from Fat 318

	% Daily Value*
Total Fat 35.3g	54%
Saturated Fat 26.5g	133%
Trans Fat 0.0g	
Cholesterol 0mg	0%
Sodium 26mg	1%
Potassium 812mg	23%
Total Carbohydrates 70.1g	23%
Dietary Fiber 10.6g	42%
Sugars 26.2g	
Protein 11.3g	

Vitamin A 1%	•	Vitamin C 24%
Calcium 6%	•	Iron 29%

Nutrition Grade B

* Based on a 2000 calorie diet

Apple oatmeal

Serves: 2

Time: 5 minutes + overnight time

Ingredients:

- 1 cup rolled oats
- 2 apples, small
- 2 tablespoons peanut butter
- 1 cup yogurt
- ½ teaspoon vanilla extract
- ¼ cup chopped pecan nuts
- 3 teaspoons honey
- 1 cup milk
- ½ teaspoon ground cinnamon

Directions:

1. Core and dice the apple.
2. In a larger Mason jar combine milk, yogurt, cinnamon and vanilla extract.
3. Add the diced apple, oats and peanut butter.
4. Stir well until combined.
5. In the morning top with pecans and drizzle with honey.
6. Serve after.

Nutrition Facts

Serving Size 496 g

Amount Per Serving

Calories 528	Calories from Fat 136

	% Daily Value*
Total Fat 15.1g	23%
Saturated Fat 4.9g	24%
Trans Fat 0.0g	
Cholesterol 17mg	6%
Sodium 221mg	9%
Potassium 813mg	23%
Total Carbohydrates 79.9g	27%
Dietary Fiber 9.8g	39%
Sugars 43.7g	
Protein 20.9g	

Vitamin A 2%	•	Vitamin C 25%
Calcium 40%	•	Iron 24%

Nutrition Grade B-

* Based on a 2000 calorie diet

Bread Pudding Based Recipes

Cinnamon bread pudding

Serves: 4

Time: 43 minutes + inactive time

Ingredients:

- 2 cups milk
- 1 loaf French bread, toasted and cubed
- 1 teaspoon cinnamon
- 1 pinch nutmeg
- 4 eggs
- 1 cup heavy cream
- ½ cup sugar

Directions:

1. Preheat oven to 350F.
2. Distribute bread cubes evenly between 4 standard Mason jars.
3. Whisk milk and heavy cream in small bowl.
4. In separate bowl whisk eggs with sugar, until pale. Add cinnamon and nutmeg.
5. Fold milk mixture into eggs and whisk until combined; pour over bread cubes until covered.
6. Arrange jars onto baking sheet and bake for 40 minutes.
7. Remove from the oven and place aside to cool for 20 minutes.
8. Serve after.

Nutrition Facts

Serving Size 222 g

Amount Per Serving

Calories 323   Calories from Fat 162

	% Daily Value*
Total Fat 18.0g	28%
Saturated Fat 9.8g	49%
Trans Fat 0.0g	
Cholesterol 215mg	72%
Sodium 131mg	5%
Potassium 154mg	4%
Total Carbohydrates 32.7g	11%
Sugars 30.9g	
Protein 10.2g	

Vitamin A 14%	•	Vitamin C 0%
Calcium 19%	•	Iron 5%

Nutrition Grade C

* Based on a 2000 calorie diet

Vegan bread pudding

Serves: 1

Time: 32 minutes + inactive time

Ingredients:

- ½ cup bread crusts, sliced into strips
- 1/3 cup soy milk
- ¼ cup silken tofu
- 1 tablespoon raisins
- 1 tablespoon maple syrup
- 1 teaspoon whole cane sugar
- ½ teaspoon cinnamon
- ¼ teaspoon pure vanilla extract

Directions:

1. Preheat oven to 350F.
2. Combine silken tofu, soy milk, maple syrup and vanilla in a bowl until blended thoroughly.
3. Fill standard Mason jar with bread crusts, up to half.
4. Add half of raisins and pour over with milk mixture until bread is covered.
5. Top with remaining raisins and bread slices.
6. Pour more liquid, until the jar is ¾ full.
7. Sprinkle with cane sugar and cinnamon.
8. Bake the pudding for 30 minutes. Place aside to chill and serve after.

Nutrition Facts

Serving Size 136 g

Amount Per Serving

Calories 153	Calories from Fat 19

	% Daily Value*
Total Fat 2.1g	3%
Trans Fat 0.0g	
Cholesterol 0mg	0%
Sodium 54mg	2%
Potassium 250mg	7%
Total Carbohydrates 30.3g	10%
Dietary Fiber 1.5g	6%
Sugars 23.9g	
Protein 4.4g	

Vitamin A 0%	•	Vitamin C 0%
Calcium 6%	•	Iron 8%

Nutrition Grade B

* Based on a 2000 calorie diet

Lemon-blueberry bread pudding

Serves: 6

Time: 35 minutes+ inactive time

Ingredients:

- ¾ cup blueberries, fresh
- 2 eggs
- ¼ cup sugar
- 1 ½ cups milk
- 1 teaspoon agave nectar
- ½ teaspoon fresh lemon juice
- 1 teaspoon lemon zest
- ½ lb. stale bread, diced
- ¼ cup mascarpone cheese
- 1 ½ tablespoons butter, melted
- ¼ cup heavy cream
- 1 teaspoon vanilla extract

Directions:

1. Preheat oven to 350F and grease six jars with some butter.
2. Beat the eggs with sugar and cheese in a large bowl.
3. Whisk in the milk, lemon zest, vanilla and lemon juice until blended. Stir in melted butter.
4. Place the bread cubes into Mason jars and pour over prepared milk mixture.
5. Allow the bread to sit for 20 minutes.
6. Stir in the blueberries and place jars onto baking sheet; bake for 30 minutes.
7. Remove the jars from the oven and place aside to cool. Meanwhile, pour heavy cream and agave nectar in another smaller Mason jar. Apply lid and shake well.
8. Pour over cooled bread pudding and serve.

Nutrition Facts

Serving Size 162 g

Amount Per Serving

Calories 247	Calories from Fat 86

	% Daily Value*
Total Fat 9.6g	15%
Saturated Fat 5.0g	25%
Trans Fat 0.0g	
Cholesterol 79mg	26%
Sodium 241mg	10%
Potassium 87mg	2%
Total Carbohydrates 31.6g	11%
Dietary Fiber 3.4g	13%
Sugars 14.0g	
Protein 11.1g	

Vitamin A 6%	•	Vitamin C 6%
Calcium 19%	•	Iron 9%

Nutrition Grade D+

* Based on a 2000 calorie diet

Caramel-banana bread pudding

Serves: 6

Time: 35 minutes + inactive time

Ingredients:

- 1 cup milk
- 2 tablespoons melted butter
- 2 bananas, small, sliced
- ½ teaspoon vanilla extract
- 6oz. French bread, cut in 1-inch squares
- 1/3 cup brown sugar
- 2 eggs, small
- ¼ teaspoon banana extract

Directions:

1. Preheat oven to 350F.
2. In a medium bowl whisk eggs, butter, sugar, vanilla and banana extract.
3. Place in the bread and stir gently. Place aside for 5 minutes.
4. Stir in 1 sliced banana and fill the Mason jars with mixture and pour over remaining milk mix until ¾ full.
5. Place the jars onto baking sheet and bake for 30 minutes.
6. Allow to cool and top with remaining banana sliced.
7. Serve after.

Nutrition Facts

Serving Size 136 g

Amount Per Serving

Calories 224	Calories from Fat 61
	% Daily Value*

	% Daily Value*
Total Fat 6.8g	10%
Saturated Fat 3.6g	18%
Cholesterol 68mg	23%
Sodium 254mg	11%
Potassium 233mg	7%
Total Carbohydrates 35.1g	12%
Dietary Fiber 1.7g	7%
Sugars 15.4g	
Protein 7.0g	

Vitamin A 4%	•	Vitamin C 6%
Calcium 8%	•	Iron 8%

Nutrition Grade C

* Based on a 2000 calorie diet

Chocolate-banana bread pudding

Serves: 6

Time: 35 minutes + inactive

Ingredients:

- 6 cups bread, torn into pieces, staled would be perfect
- ½ cup sugar
- 2 teaspoons pure vanilla extract
- ¼ cup butter, melted
- 1 cup dark chocolate chips
- 2 eggs
- 2 cups milk

Directions:

1. Place bread pieces in a bowl; add chocolate chips.
2. In separate bowl combine melted butter, eggs and milk. Add sugar and stir until sugar is dissolved.
3. Pour the milk mixture over bread pieces and place aside 60 minutes.
4. Spoon bread into Mason jars and transfer the jars onto baking sheet.
5. Pour boiling water. Around 1-inch over jars and bake for 25 minutes.
6. Place aside to cool before serving.

Nutrition Facts

Serving Size 179 g

Amount Per Serving

Calories 382	Calories from Fat 156
	% Daily Value*
Total Fat 17.3g	27%
Saturated Fat 9.9g	49%
Cholesterol 82mg	27%
Sodium 352mg	15%
Potassium 106mg	3%
Total Carbohydrates 52.0g	17%
Dietary Fiber 0.8g	3%
Sugars 32.8g	
Protein 8.6g	

Vitamin A 7%	•	Vitamin C 0%
Calcium 16%	•	Iron 11%

Nutrition Grade D

* Based on a 2000 calorie diet

Pumpkin bread pudding

Serves: 2

Time: 25 minutes + inactive time

Ingredients:

- 2 cups bread pieces, staled bread is perfect
- 1 egg
- ¾ cup milk
- ¾ cup pumpkin puree
- ½ teaspoon vanilla extract
- 1 teaspoon pumpkin pie spice
- 1/3 cup brown sugar

Directions:

1. Preheat oven to 350F.
2. In a large bowl whisk together the egg, milk, pumpkin puree, vanilla, sugar and pumpkin spice.
3. Add bread pieces and stir to combine. Place aside for 20 minutes.
4. Fill the Mason jars with prepared, up to ¾ full.
5. Place the jars onto baking sheet and bake for 20 minutes.
6. Remove from the oven and allow cooling before serving.

Nutrition Facts

Serving Size 331 g

Amount Per Serving

Calories 206	Calories from Fat 40
	% Daily Value*
Total Fat 4.4g	7%
Saturated Fat 2.0g	10%
Cholesterol 89mg	30%
Sodium 86mg	4%
Potassium 311mg	9%
Total Carbohydrates 36.5g	12%
Dietary Fiber 2.8g	11%
Sugars 31.0g	
Protein 6.9g	

Vitamin A 289%	•	Vitamin C 7%
Calcium 17%	•	Iron 11%

Nutrition Grade C+

* Based on a 2000 calorie diet

Strawberry bread pudding

Serves: 6

Time: 35 minutes + inactive time

Ingredients:

- ½ lb. fresh strawberries, quartered
- ½ lb. stale bread, cut into 1-inch dices
- ¾ cup brown sugar
- 3 eggs
- Small pinch salt
- ½ cup heavy cream
- ½ teaspoon vanilla extract
- 2 cups milk

For the topping:

- ¼ cup crème fraiche
- ½ cup heavy cream
- ½ tablespoon brown sugar

Directions:

1. In a large bowl whisk eggs, sugar, salt, heavy cream, vanilla and milk.
2. Add bread and stir to combine. Place aside for 1 hour.
3. Coat six Mason jars with some butter and place onto baking sheet.
4. Stir strawberries into bread mixture and fill the jars up to ¾ full.
5. Bake bread pudding for 30 minutes. Remove from the oven and place aside to cool.
6. Meanwhile, whip the crème fraiche, heavy cream and brown sugar in a bowl.
7. When bread pudding is cooled, top with whipped crème fraiche and serve.

Nutrition Facts

Serving Size 189 g

Amount Per Serving	
Calories 226	Calories from Fat 102

	% Daily Value*
Total Fat 11.4g	17%
Saturated Fat 6.3g	31%
Cholesterol 116mg	39%
Sodium 82mg	3%
Potassium 175mg	5%
Total Carbohydrates 26.2g	9%
Dietary Fiber 0.8g	3%
Sugars 24.1g	
Protein 6.1g	

Vitamin A 8%	•	Vitamin C 37%
Calcium 14%	•	Iron 4%

Nutrition Grade C

* Based on a 2000 calorie diet

Tres leche bread pudding

Serves: 4

Time: 40 minutes + inactive time

Ingredients:

- ½ cup milk
- 7oz. condensed milk
- 6oz. evaporated milk
- 1/3 cup sugar
- 2 eggs, small
- 1 egg yolk
- ½ teaspoon vanilla
- 2 croissants, cut into cubes

Directions:

1. In a sauce pan combine milk, condensed milk, evaporated milk, sugar, eggs, egg yolk and vanilla.
2. Bring to simmer over medium heat and simmer for 2 minutes.
3. Stir in croissant cubes and place aside for 10 minutes.
4. Transfer the content into Mason jars, to ¾ full.
5. Place the jars into baking pan and fill around with water, around 1 ½ -inches.
6. Bake the pudding for 35 minutes at 375F.
7. Remove from the oven and when cooled, serve.

Nutrition Facts

Serving Size 200 g

Amount Per Serving

Calories 476	Calories from Fat 167

	% Daily Value*
Total Fat 18.5g	28%
Saturated Fat 10.1g	50%
Cholesterol 188mg	63%
Sodium 405mg	17%
Potassium 405mg	12%
Total Carbohydrates 65.2g	22%
Dietary Fiber 0.9g	3%
Sugars 53.3g	
Protein 14.0g	

Vitamin A 13%	•	Vitamin C 4%
Calcium 32%	•	Iron 8%

Nutrition Grade C-

* Based on a 2000 calorie diet

Sweet potato bread pudding

Serves: 3

Time: 45 minutes + inactive time

Ingredients:

- 3 cups corn bread, cut into 1-inch pieces, toasted
- 1 egg, lightly beaten
- ¾ cup milk
- 1 tablespoon brown sugar
- 1 sweet potato, baked and mashed
- ¼ cup pecan nuts, chopped
- ½ teaspoon cinnamon
- ¼ teaspoon nutmeg
- 2 tablespoons shredded coconut
- 2 tablespoon butter, buttered

For the coconut sauce:

- 7oz. coconut milk
- 2 tablespoons sugar
- 1 teaspoon cornstarch
- 1 tablespoon water
- 1 teaspoon lime juice

Directions:

1. Preheat oven to 350F.
2. Combine cornbread and pecan nuts in a bowl. Fold in mashed sweet potato.
3. In separate bowl whisk eggs, milk, sugar, cinnamon and nutmeg. Fold bread mixture into milk and let it stand for 5 minutes. Fill Mason jars with prepared mixture and pour over remaining liquid. Place the jars onto baking sheet and bake in the preheated oven for 20 minutes.
4. Meanwhile, prepare the sauce; combine the coconut milk, lime juice and sugar. Bring the mixture to boil; reduce heat to medium

and simmer until sugar dissolves. Combine starch with water and fold in coconut milk mixture. Simmer until sauce is slightly thickened for 2 minutes. Remove the Mason jars from the oven and when cooled drizzle with coconut sauce. Serve after.

Nutrition Facts

Serving Size 210 g

Amount Per Serving

Calories 364	Calories from Fat 247
	% Daily Value*
Total Fat 27.4g	42%
Saturated Fat 21.1g	105%
Trans Fat 0.0g	
Cholesterol 80mg	27%
Sodium 129mg	5%
Potassium 430mg	12%
Total Carbohydrates 27.3g	9%
Dietary Fiber 3.3g	13%
Sugars 18.7g	
Protein 6.3g	

Vitamin A 9%	•	Vitamin C 24%
Calcium 10%	•	Iron 18%

Nutrition Grade B

* Based on a 2000 calorie diet

Chestnut bread pudding

Serves: 4

Time: 40 minutes + inactive time

Ingredients:

- 2 eggs
- 1 ¾ cups heavy cream
- ¾ loaf egg bread, diced in 1-ich cubes
- ¾ cup milk
- 1/3 cup oat flakes
- ¾ teaspoon cinnamon
- ¾ teaspoon pure vanilla
- ¼ cup chestnut spread

Directions:

1. Beat eggs with milk, heavy cream, vanilla and chestnut spread in a bowl.
2. Toss bread with cinnamon and oats in separate bowl; fold into egg mixture and refrigerate for 1 hour.
3. Preheat oven to 350F.
4. Transfer the mixture into Mason jars, to ¾ full.
5. Arrange the jars onto baking sheet and bake in preheated oven for 35 minutes.
6. Place aside to cool before serving.

Nutrition Facts

Serving Size 140 g

Amount Per Serving

Calories 282	Calories from Fat 218
	% Daily Value*
Total Fat 24.2g	37%
Saturated Fat 13.8g	69%
Trans Fat 0.0g	
Cholesterol 198mg	66%
Sodium 88mg	4%
Potassium 140mg	4%
Total Carbohydrates 9.2g	3%
Dietary Fiber 1.1g	4%
Sugars 2.4g	
Protein 7.9g	

Vitamin A 19%	•	Vitamin C 1%
Calcium 11%	•	Iron 6%

Nutrition Grade B-

* Based on a 2000 calorie diet

Parfait Based Recipes

Fruity parfait with nutty granola

Serves: 2

Time: 30 minutes

Ingredients:

- ½ cup rolled oats
- ¼ cup walnuts, chopped
- 1 teaspoon butter
- 2 tablespoons maple syrup, divided
- ¾ cup mango, peeled and diced
- 1 cup yogurt
- ½ cup kiwi, peeled and diced
- ½ cup blueberries, fresh

Directions:

1. Mix oats and walnuts and place onto baking pan.
2. Combine half of the maple syrup and butter in small sauce pan; bring to boil and pour over nuts and oats.
3. Shake to combine and bake in preheated oven for 20 minutes at 375F, stirring occasionally.
4. Let the granola cool before using.
5. Gently toss fruits with remaining syrup and divide fruits between 2 Mason jars.
6. Sprinkle each parfait with granola, equally and top with equal amount of yogurt.
7. Serve and enjoy.

Nutrition Facts

Serving Size 261 g

Amount Per Serving

Calories 378	Calories from Fat 129

	% Daily Value*
Total Fat 14.4g	22%
Saturated Fat 3.2g	16%
Cholesterol 12mg	4%
Sodium 104mg	4%
Potassium 650mg	19%
Total Carbohydrates 49.2g	16%
Dietary Fiber 5.3g	21%
Sugars 28.5g	
Protein 14.2g	

Vitamin A 3%	•	Vitamin C 80%
Calcium 27%	•	Iron 13%

Nutrition Grade A-

* Based on a 2000 calorie diet

Banana split parfait

Serves: 4

Time: 10 minutes

Ingredients:

- 1 cup heavy cream
- 1 cup strawberries, sliced
- 1 cup bananas, sliced
- ½ cup walnuts, crushed
- ½ teaspoon vanilla bean paste
- 3 teaspoons cocoa powder
- 2 teaspoons powdered sugar
- ½ teaspoon corn flour
- 4 teaspoons milk

Directions:

1. Whip together heavy cream, corn flour and vanilla paste. Place in a refrigerator until ready to use.
2. In a small bowl combine milk, cocoa powder and powdered sugar. Place aside.
3. Layer Mason jars with ¼ whipped cream, ¼ chocolate sauce, ¼ strawberries, ¼ bananas and ¼ walnuts.
4. Refrigerate the parfait for 10 minutes and serve after.

Nutrition Facts

Serving Size 127 g

Amount Per Serving

Calories 256   Calories from Fat 188

	% Daily Value*
Total Fat 20.8g	32%
Saturated Fat 7.6g	38%
Cholesterol 42mg	14%
Sodium 15mg	1%
Potassium 331mg	9%
Total Carbohydrates 16.2g	5%
Dietary Fiber 3.2g	13%
Sugars 8.0g	
Protein 5.5g	

Vitamin A 10%	•	Vitamin C 41%
Calcium 4%	•	Iron 5%

Nutrition Grade B

* Based on a 2000 calorie diet

Paleo Parfait

Serves: 2

Time: 10 minutes

Ingredients:

- ½ cup pecans, crushed
- 1 apple, cored and diced
- 4 dates, pitted
- ¼ cup coconut flakes
- 1 teaspoon pure vanilla
- 2 teaspoons cinnamon
- 2 tablespoons maple syrup, divided
- Pinch of salt
- 1 cup coconut cream

Directions:

1. Place the dates and diced apple into a small sauce pan. Add 1/3 cup water and bring to gentle simmer.
2. Simmer the apples until tender and transfer into food processor.
3. Puree the apples until smooth, adding water if needed. Place aside.
4. Clean the processor and place pecans and coconut in the processor; pulse until combined.
5. Transfer to a pan and sprinkle with cinnamon and add half of maple syrup. Cook on low heat until pecans are toasted. Place aside.
6. Whisk together remaining maple syrup with coconut cream and assemble the parfait; place some of the coconut cream in Mason jar. Add thin layer of apples and sprinkle with thin layer of pecans.
7. Continue layering until the top of Mason jar is reached. Serve immediately.

Nutrition Facts

Serving Size 260 g

Amount Per Serving

Calories 463	Calories from Fat 290

	% Daily Value*
Total Fat 32.2g	50%
Saturated Fat 28.4g	142%
Trans Fat 0.0g	
Cholesterol 0mg	0%
Sodium 101mg	4%
Potassium 608mg	17%
Total Carbohydrates 48.5g	16%
Dietary Fiber 8.3g	33%
Sugars 36.6g	
Protein 3.8g	

Vitamin A 0%	•	Vitamin C 18%
Calcium 6%	•	Iron 24%

Nutrition Grade B-

* Based on a 2000 calorie diet

Yogurt breakfast parfait

Serves: 1

Time: 10 minutes + inactive time

Ingredients:

- 6oz. Greek yogurt
- 1 tablespoon chia seeds
- 1/3 cup rolled oats
- 1 cup mixed berries, frozen
- 2 tablespoons almond milk

Directions:

1. Combine oats, yogurt and milk in a bowl.
2. Transfer half of mixture into Mason jar.
3. Top with half of the berries and remaining yogurt mix.
4. Finally top with remaining berries and store in refrigerator overnight.
5. Serve in the morning.

Nutrition Facts

Serving Size 375 g

Amount Per Serving	
Calories 409	Calories from Fat 138

	% Daily Value*
Total Fat 15.3g	24%
Saturated Fat 9.4g	47%
Trans Fat 0.0g	
Cholesterol 9mg	3%
Sodium 61mg	3%
Potassium 647mg	18%
Total Carbohydrates 46.9g	16%
Dietary Fiber 10.9g	44%
Sugars 18.1g	
Protein 23.8g	

Vitamin A 2%	•	Vitamin C 52%
Calcium 27%	•	Iron 17%

Nutrition Grade B
* Based on a 2000 calorie diet

Mocha-oatmeal breakfast parfait

Serves: 2

Time: 10 minutes + inactive time

Ingredients:

- 1 banana, sliced
- 1 cup rolled oats
- 1 cup milk
- 1 tablespoon chia seeds
- 1 tablespoon cacao powder
- 2 teaspoons maple syrup
- 1 tablespoon walnuts, crushed
- 1 shot warm espresso
- 1/8 teaspoon cinnamon

Directions:

1. Add ½ cup of the milk, cacao powder and espresso to blender.
2. Blend on low until smooth.
3. Once the cacao is dissolved, add in the remaining milk, maple syrup and cinnamon.
4. Combine chia seeds, oats and milk mixture in a jar.
5. Add sliced banana and crushed walnuts.
6. Place in the refrigerator overnight and serve in the morning.

Nutrition Facts

Serving Size 239 g

Amount Per Serving

Calories 330	Calories from Fat 83

	% Daily Value*
Total Fat 9.2g	14%
Saturated Fat 2.2g	11%
Trans Fat 0.0g	
Cholesterol 10mg	3%
Sodium 61mg	3%
Potassium 489mg	14%
Total Carbohydrates 55.1g	18%
Dietary Fiber 8.2g	33%
Sugars 17.1g	
Protein 11.7g	

Vitamin A 1%	•	Vitamin C 9%
Calcium 21%	•	Iron 14%

Nutrition Grade A

* Based on a 2000 calorie diet

Cookie dough parfait

Serves: 1

Time: 15 minutes

Ingredients:

For the cookie dough:

- ¼ banana, large, sliced
- ¼ banana, mashed
- 1 ½ tablespoons crunchy peanut butter
- ½ cup quick oats, divided
- ½ cup Greek yogurt
- ½ tablespoon milk

Directions:

1. Prepare the cookie dough; process half of the quick oats in food processor until you get fine flour.
2. Pour flour into bowl and add remaining oats. In separate bowl blend peanut butter and milk. Stir in mashed banana.
3. Blend quick oats with peanut butter mixture and stir until you get dough consistency.
4. Layer cookie dough, Greek yogurt and sliced bananas; repeat the layers until Mason jar is full. Serve immediately.

Nutrition Facts

Serving Size 250 g

Amount Per Serving

Calories 441	Calories from Fat 157

	% Daily Value*
Total Fat 17.5g	27%
Saturated Fat 4.9g	25%
Trans Fat 0.0g	
Cholesterol 7mg	2%
Sodium 155mg	6%
Potassium 686mg	20%
Total Carbohydrates 51.0g	17%
Dietary Fiber 7.1g	28%
Sugars 14.9g	
Protein 24.1g	

Vitamin A 2%	•	Vitamin C 9%
Calcium 15%	•	Iron 23%

Nutrition Grade B

* Based on a 2000 calorie diet

Cereal parfait

Serves: 1

Time: 5 minutes

Ingredients:

- ¼ cup cereals, like Cherrios
- ¼ cup cluster granola
- ½ cup quinoa, cooked
- 4 teaspoons honey
- ½ cup thick yogurt
- ½ cup blueberries, fresh, slightly mashed

Directions:

1. Combine thick yogurt with quinoa and honey in a small bowl.
2. Layer half of the yogurt into standard Mason jar.
3. Cover with half of the cereals, half of cluster granola and half of the blueberries.
4. Repeat layers and serve.

Nutrition Facts

Serving Size 200 g

Amount Per Serving

Calories 487	Calories from Fat 51

	% Daily Value*
Total Fat 5.7g	9%
Saturated Fat 0.7g	3%
Trans Fat 0.0g	
Cholesterol 0mg	0%
Sodium 64mg	3%
Potassium 631mg	18%
Total Carbohydrates 99.6g	33%
Dietary Fiber 9.8g	39%
Sugars 35.4g	
Protein 13.9g	

Vitamin A 0%	•	Vitamin C 19%	
Calcium 5%	•	Iron 43%	

Nutrition Grade A
* Based on a 2000 calorie diet

Popped amaranth parfait

Serves: 2

Time: 5 minutes

Ingredients:

- 1 cup popped amaranth (pop them like pop-corns)
- 5 strawberries, fresh, sliced
- 1 cup yogurt
- 1 banana, sliced
- ½ cup quinoa, cooked

Directions:

1. Distribute the quinoa in the bottom of a two Mason jars.
2. Top with layer of yogurt, layer of popped amaranth, bananas and sliced strawberries, dividing evenly between the jars.
3. Serve immediately.

Nutrition Facts

Serving Size 251 g

Amount Per Serving	
Calories 303	Calories from Fat 39

	% Daily Value*
Total Fat 4.3g	7%
Saturated Fat 1.6g	8%
Cholesterol 7mg	2%
Sodium 87mg	4%
Potassium 775mg	22%
Total Carbohydrates 51.4g	17%
Dietary Fiber 5.1g	20%
Sugars 17.1g	
Protein 13.6g	

Vitamin A 2%	•	Vitamin C 40%
Calcium 25%	•	Iron 13%

Nutrition Grade A-

* Based on a 2000 calorie diet

Apple-pear parfait

Serves: 2

Time: 35 minutes

Ingredients:

- 1 cup yogurt
- 1 tablespoon honey
- 1 pear, peeled and diced
- 2 apples, peeled, cored and diced
- 1 tablespoon brown sugar
- ¾ teaspoon cinnamon

Directions:

1. Preheat oven to 400F and line baking sheet with parchment paper.
2. In a bowl toss fruits with ¼ teaspoon cinnamon and brown sugar; transfer onto baking sheet in a single layer.
3. Bake for 20 minutes.
4. Meanwhile, combine yogurt with honey and remaining cinnamon.
5. Place the two tablespoons of the apple mixture in the bottom of Mason jar.
6. Top with 2 tablespoon yogurt and repeat layers in two Mason jars.
7. Serve after.

Nutrition Facts

Serving Size 386 g

Amount Per Serving

Calories 271	Calories from Fat 17
	% Daily Value*
Total Fat 1.9g	3%
Saturated Fat 1.2g	6%
Trans Fat 0.0g	
Cholesterol 7mg	2%
Sodium 88mg	4%
Potassium 569mg	16%
Total Carbohydrates 57.8g	19%
Dietary Fiber 7.0g	28%
Sugars 47.1g	
Protein 7.6g	

Vitamin A 2%	•	Vitamin C 30%
Calcium 24%	•	Iron 7%

Nutrition Grade A

* Based on a 2000 calorie diet

Quinoa parfait

Serves: 2

Time: 15 minutes + inactive time

Ingredients:

- 2 apples, peeled, cored and diced
- ½ teaspoon cinnamon
- ½ cup water
- ½ teaspoon vanilla
- 1 cup cooked quinoa
- ½ cup yogurt

Directions:

1. In a medium sauce pan combine water, apples, cinnamon and vanilla.
2. Bring to simmer over medium heat.
3. Simmer for 10 minutes or until apples are tender.
4. Place ¼ cup yogurt in the bottom of Mason jar. Top with ½ cup quinoa and ½ apple mixture.
5. Repeat with remaining ingredients in second Mason jar.

Nutrition Facts

Serving Size 389 g

Amount Per Serving

Calories 456   Calories from Fat 56

	% Daily Value*
Total Fat 6.2g	10%
Saturated Fat 1.2g	6%
Trans Fat 0.0g	
Cholesterol 4mg	1%
Sodium 51mg	2%
Potassium 821mg	23%
Total Carbohydrates 84.6g	28%
Dietary Fiber 10.7g	43%
Sugars 23.4g	
Protein 16.0g	

Vitamin A 1%	•	Vitamin C 24%
Calcium 16%	•	Iron 27%

Nutrition Grade B-

* Based on a 2000 calorie diet

Pancake Based Recipes

Blueberry pancakes in a jar

Serves: 2

Time: 5 minutes

Ingredients:

- ½ cup all-purpose flour
- 1/3 cup milk
- ¼ cup blueberries, fresh
- ½ teaspoon baking powder
- 1 tablespoon sugar
- 1 tablespoon butter, melted
- 1 tablespoon maple syrup

Directions:

1. Combine flour, baking powder and sugar in a small bowl.
2. Stir in melted butter and milk until blended.
3. Divide blueberries between two Mason jars, at the bottom and pour over prepared batter.
4. Microwave pancaked for 60 seconds and drizzle with maple syrup before serving.

Nutrition Facts

Serving Size 114 g

Amount Per Serving

Calories 245 | Calories from Fat 63

	% Daily Value*
Total Fat 7.0g	11%
Saturated Fat 4.2g	21%
Cholesterol 19mg	6%
Sodium 63mg	3%
Potassium 219mg	6%
Total Carbohydrates 41.8g	14%
Dietary Fiber 1.3g	5%
Sugars 15.7g	
Protein 4.8g	

Vitamin A 4%	•	Vitamin C 5%
Calcium 12%	•	Iron 11%

Nutrition Grade B-

* Based on a 2000 calorie diet

Banana pancakes in a jar

Serves: 1

Time: 4 minutes

Ingredients:

- ½ tablespoon peanut butter
- ½ tablespoon honey
- ½ cup flour, whole wheat
- ¼ cup milk + 1 tablespoon
- 1 teaspoon baking powder
- ¼ teaspoon cinnamon
- 1/8 teaspoon banana extract
- 1 banana, medium

Directions:

1. Combine flour, cinnamon and baking powder in a bowl.
2. In separate bowl whisk the milk, banana extract, honey and peanut butter. Fold into flour mix and stir until blended thoroughly.
3. Dice half of the banana and place in the bottom of Mason jar.
4. Spoon the batter over bananas and microwave for 90-10 seconds, on high.
5. Top with remaining bananas and additionally drizzle with honey.

Nutrition Facts

Serving Size 266 g

Amount Per Serving

Calories 450	Calories from Fat 57

	% Daily Value*
Total Fat 6.3g	10%
Saturated Fat 1.8g	9%
Trans Fat 0.0g	
Cholesterol 5mg	2%
Sodium 73mg	3%
Potassium 1090mg	31%
Total Carbohydrates 90.8g	30%
Dietary Fiber 5.7g	23%
Sugars 26.8g	
Protein 11.8g	

Vitamin A 2%	•	Vitamin C 17%
Calcium 31%	•	Iron 25%

Nutrition Grade B

* Based on a 2000 calorie diet

Raspberry pancakes in a jar

Serves: 1

Time: 5 minutes

Ingredients:

- ½ cup all-purpose flour
- 1 tablespoon sugar
- ¼ cup raspberries, fresh
- ¼ cup raspberry syrup
- 1 tablespoon butter, melted
- ½ tablespoon baking powder
- ¼ + 1 tablespoon almond milk

Directions:

1. Whisk the flour, baking powder and sugar in small bowl.
2. Stir in milk and melted butter; continue stirring until combined thoroughly.
3. Cover the bottom of a Mason jar with raspberries; spoon over prepared batter and microwave 60 seconds.
4. Top with additional butter and raspberry syrup before serving.

Nutrition Facts

Serving Size 188 g

Amount Per Serving

Calories 428	Calories from Fat 122

	% Daily Value*
Total Fat 13.6g	21%
Saturated Fat 8.2g	41%
Cholesterol 36mg	12%
Sodium 119mg	5%
Potassium 909mg	26%
Total Carbohydrates 69.9g	23%
Dietary Fiber 3.9g	15%
Sugars 16.3g	
Protein 9.0g	

Vitamin A 8%	•	Vitamin C 13%
Calcium 42%	•	Iron 21%

Nutrition Grade B

* Based on a 2000 calorie diet

Red velvet pancakes in a jar

Serves: 1

Time: 4 minutes

Ingredients:

- ½ cup flour
- ½ tablespoon baking powder
- ½ teaspoon red food coloring
- ¼ cup + 1 tablespoon milk
- 1 teaspoon cocoa powder
- ¼ teaspoon vanilla extract
- 1 tablespoon butter, melted
- 1 tablespoon sugar

For the glaze:

- 2 tablespoons cream cheese, softened
- ½ tablespoon butter, softened
- ¼ tablespoon milk
- 1 tablespoon powdered sugar
- 1/8 teaspoon vanilla extract

Directions:

1. In a small bowl whisk together the flour, cocoa powder, baking powder and sugar.
2. Fold in milk, butter, vanilla extract and red food coloring; stir well until combined.
3. Spoon the batter into Mason jar and microwave for 60-80 seconds on high.
4. Meanwhile, whisk together the glaze ingredients.
5. Spoon the glaze over pancake and serve.

Nutrition Facts

Serving Size 141 g

Amount Per Serving	
Calories 544	Calories from Fat 227

	% Daily Value*
Total Fat 25.2g	39%
Saturated Fat 15.6g	78%
Cholesterol 68mg	23%
Sodium 192mg	8%
Potassium 903mg	26%
Total Carbohydrates 73.1g	24%
Dietary Fiber 2.4g	10%
Sugars 20.4g	
Protein 8.6g	

Vitamin A 16%	•	Vitamin C 0%	
Calcium 36%	•	Iron 22%	

Nutrition Grade C-

* Based on a 2000 calorie diet

Oatmeal pancakes

Serves: 1

Time: 5 minutes + inactive time

Ingredients:

- ½ cup rolled oats
- ¼ cup buttermilk + 1 tablespoon
- 1 tablespoon butter, melted
- ½ tablespoon plain flour
- 1 teaspoon baking powder
- ¼ teaspoon cinnamon
- 2 tablespoons crushed pecans

Directions:

1. Mix rolled oats and buttermilk in a bowl; cover and store in refrigerator overnight.
2. In the morning, combine flour, baking powder and cinnamon in a bowl.
3. Add oats mixture, along with melted butter.
4. Spoon the batter into Mason jar and top with pecan nuts.
5. Microwave for 80-90 seconds on high.
6. Serve after, with a scoop of vanilla ice cream.

Nutrition Facts

Serving Size 126 g

Amount Per Serving

Calories 302	Calories from Fat 133

	% Daily Value*
Total Fat 14.8g	23%
Saturated Fat 8.1g	40%
Trans Fat 0.0g	
Cholesterol 33mg	11%
Sodium 153mg	6%
Potassium 756mg	22%
Total Carbohydrates 36.4g	12%
Dietary Fiber 4.7g	19%
Sugars 3.4g	
Protein 8.0g	

Vitamin A 7%	•	Vitamin C 1%
Calcium 32%	•	Iron 13%

Nutrition Grade B

* Based on a 2000 calorie diet

Whole wheat chocolate chip pancakes

Serves: 2

Time: 5 minutes

Ingredients:

- 1 cup whole wheat flour
- ¼ cup mini dark chocolate chips
- 2 tablespoons sugar
- 2 tablespoons melted butter
- ¾ cup milk
- 1 tablespoon baking powder
- 2 tablespoons old fashioned oats
- Very small pinch salt

Directions:

1. Place oats in food processor and pulse until finely chopped, not powdered.
2. Add in flour, sugar and baking powder; pulse few times until blended.
3. Using paddle attachment blend in milk, melted butter and salt.
4. Spoon the batter into two Mason jars and sprinkle with chocolate chips.
5. Microwave the batter for 90 seconds on high.
6. Serve after.

Nutrition Facts

Serving Size 490 g

Amount Per Serving

Calories 933   Calories from Fat 264

	% Daily Value*
Total Fat 29.4g	45%
Saturated Fat 17.3g	86%
Trans Fat 0.0g	
Cholesterol 76mg	25%
Sodium 266mg	11%
Potassium 1847mg	53%
Total Carbohydrates 148.9g	50%
Dietary Fiber 5.7g	23%
Sugars 33.1g	
Protein 21.7g	

Vitamin A 15%	•	Vitamin C 0%
Calcium 90%	•	Iron 44%

Nutrition Grade B

* Based on a 2000 calorie diet

Double vanilla pancakes

Serves: 1

Time: 5 minutes

Ingredients:

For the vanilla glaze:

- ¼ teaspoon pure vanilla paste
- ¼ cup cream cheese, softened
- 1 tablespoon butter, softened
- 1 tablespoon icing sugar

For the pancakes:

- ½ cup flour, all purpose
- ¼ cup vanilla chips
- ½ tablespoon baking powder
- 1 tablespoon melted butter
- 1 tablespoon brown sugar
- ¼ cup buttermilk + 1 tablespoon

Directions:

1. Prepare the glaze; cream the cheese, sugar, vanilla and butter in a bowl. Place aside.
2. In small bowl blend flour, baking powder and sugar.
3. Stir in the butter milk and gently fold vanilla chips.
4. Transfer the batter into Mason jar and microwave in high for 70 seconds.
5. Top with prepared glaze before serving.

Nutrition Facts

Serving Size 145 g

Amount Per Serving

Calories 503	Calories from Fat 188

% Daily Value*

Total Fat 20.9g	32%
Saturated Fat 12.8g	64%
Cholesterol 64mg	21%
Sodium 182mg	8%
Potassium 906mg	26%
Total Carbohydrates 69.5g	23%
Dietary Fiber 1.9g	7%
Sugars 16.9g	
Protein 10.9g	

Vitamin A 16%	•	Vitamin C 0%
Calcium 39%	•	Iron 24%

Nutrition Grade C+

* Based on a 2000 calorie diet

Cinnamon swirl pancakes

Serves: 1

Time: 5 minutes

Ingredients:

For the pancakes:

- ½ cup flour
- ½ tablespoon baking powder
- 1 tablespoon sugar
- 1 tablespoon melted butter
- 1/8 teaspoon vanilla

For the swirl:

- ½ tablespoon butter, melted
- 1 tablespoon brown sugar
- 2 teaspoons ground cinnamon

Directions:

1. Prepare the swirl; whisk all ingredients until blended and spoon into small piping bag, with plain nozzle. Place aside.
2. Prepare the pancakes; whisk together flour, baking powder and sugar.
3. Stir in melted butter and milk, along with vanilla. Stir until blended thoroughly.
4. Spoon the batter into Mason jar and pipe the cinnamon mix in swirl motion over batter.
5. Microwave the pancake for 80-90 seconds and serve faster.

Nutrition Facts

Serving Size 103 g

Amount Per Serving

Calories 378	Calories from Fat 58
	% Daily Value*
Total Fat 6.5g	10%
Saturated Fat 3.8g	19%
Trans Fat 0.0g	
Cholesterol 15mg	5%
Sodium 52mg	2%
Potassium 859mg	25%
Total Carbohydrates 75.8g	25%
Dietary Fiber 4.3g	17%
Sugars 21.1g	
Protein 6.7g	

Vitamin A 4%	•	Vitamin C 0%
Calcium 39%	•	Iron 22%

Nutrition Grade C
* Based on a 2000 calorie diet

Banana-chocolate pancakes

Serves: 2

Time: 5 minutes

Ingredients:

- 1 cup all-purpose flour
- 1 tablespoon sugar
- 1 ½ tablespoons vegetable oil
- ½ tablespoon cocoa powder
- ½ tablespoon baking powder
- ½ banana, small, mashed
- ¼ teaspoon vanilla extract
- ¾ cup buttermilk
- Very small pinch salt

Directions:

1. In a small bowl whisk flour, sugar, cocoa powder, baking powder and salt.
2. In separate bowl whisk buttermilk, oil, mashed banana and vanilla extract. Fold liquid ingredients into flour mixture and stir until blended.
3. Spoon the mixture into two Mason jars and microwave for 90 seconds.
4. Serve after.

Nutrition Facts

Serving Size 206 g

Amount Per Serving

Calories 411   Calories from Fat 107

	% Daily Value*
Total Fat 11.9g	18%
Saturated Fat 2.7g	14%
Cholesterol 4mg	1%
Sodium 102mg	4%
Potassium 725mg	21%
Total Carbohydrates 67.4g	22%
Dietary Fiber 2.9g	12%
Sugars 14.3g	
Protein 10.1g	

Vitamin A 1%	•	Vitamin C 6%
Calcium 28%	•	Iron 20%

Nutrition Grade C+

* Based on a 2000 calorie diet

Gluten-free pancakes

Serves: 1

Time: 3 minutes

Ingredients:

- 1 large banana, mashed
- 1 egg
- ¼ cup blueberries
- ¼ teaspoon cinnamon

Directions:

1. Mash the banana in a bowl.
2. Whisk in egg, cinnamon and whisk all until blended.
3. Spoon half of the batter in a Mason jar, top with half of blueberries and layer with remaining batter.
4. Microwave for 90-120 seconds and serve with remaining fresh blueberries.

Nutrition Facts

Serving Size 261 g

Amount Per Serving	
Calories 269	Calories from Fat 84

	% Daily Value*
Total Fat 9.3g	14%
Saturated Fat 2.9g	14%
Trans Fat 0.0g	
Cholesterol 327mg	109%
Sodium 125mg	5%
Potassium 635mg	18%
Total Carbohydrates 37.5g	12%
Dietary Fiber 4.7g	19%
Sugars 20.9g	
Protein 12.8g	

Vitamin A 10%	•	Vitamin C 29%	
Calcium 6%	•	Iron 14%	

Nutrition Grade A-
* Based on a 2000 calorie diet

Made in the USA
Las Vegas, NV
07 September 2023